Gorillas

Kate Riggs

Published by Creative Paperbacks
P.O. Box 227, Mankato, Minnesota 56002
Creative Paperbacks is an imprint of
The Creative Company
www.thecreativecompany.us

Design and production by Ellen Huber
Art direction by Rita Marshall
Printed in the United States of America

Photographs by Getty Images (Ian Nichols, Joel Sartore,
Peter G. Veit/National Geographic), iStockphoto
(DaveThomasNZ, Guenter Guni, Eric Isselée, Marcel Mooij,
Prill Mediendesign & Fotografie), Shutterstock (Aaron Amat,
BGSmith, Eric Isselee, emin kuliyev, Marek Velechovsky),
SuperStock (Philip Lee Harvey/Cultura Limited)

Library of Congress Cataloging-in-Publication Data
Riggs, Kate.
Gorillas / Kate Riggs.
p. cm. — (Seedlings)
Includes bibliographical references and index.
Summary: A kindergarten-level introduction to gorillas,
covering their growth process, behaviors, the forests
they call home, and such defining physical features as
their strong jaws.
ISBN 978-1-60818-454-5 (hardcover)
ISBN 978-1-62832-043-5 (pbk)
1. Gorilla—Juvenile literature. I. Title.

QL737.P96R542 2014
599.884—dc23   2013029068

CCSS: RI.K.1, 2, 3, 4, 5, 6, 7;
RI.1.1, 2, 3, 4, 5, 6, 7; RF.K.1, 3; RF.1.1

First Edition
9 8 7 6 5 4 3 2 1

TABLE OF CONTENTS

Hello, gorillas!

Gorillas are animals called apes.

They live in forests in Africa.

Gorillas are big.
They have
hairy bodies.

They have large heads.

A gorilla has long arms.

It uses its hands
and feet to walk.

Gorillas love to eat plants. They have strong jaws. Gorillas make many sounds. They grunt and bark.

13

A young gorilla
is called a baby.
Babies live with
their family in
a troop.

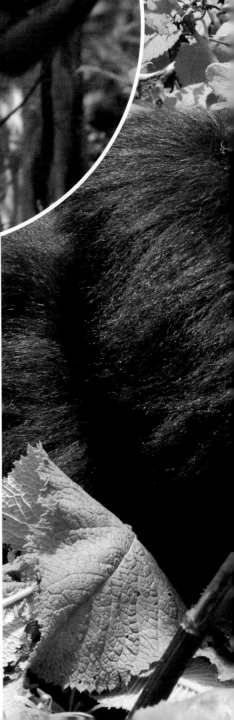

All the gorillas eat and eat. Then they take a nap. Baby gorillas play.

Goodbye, gorillas!

Picture a Gorilla

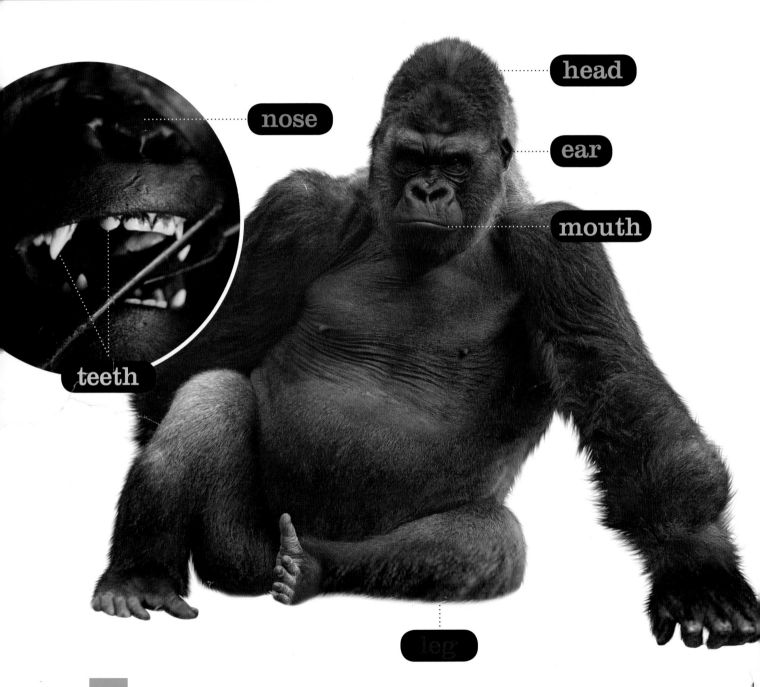

nose

head

ear

mouth

teeth

leg

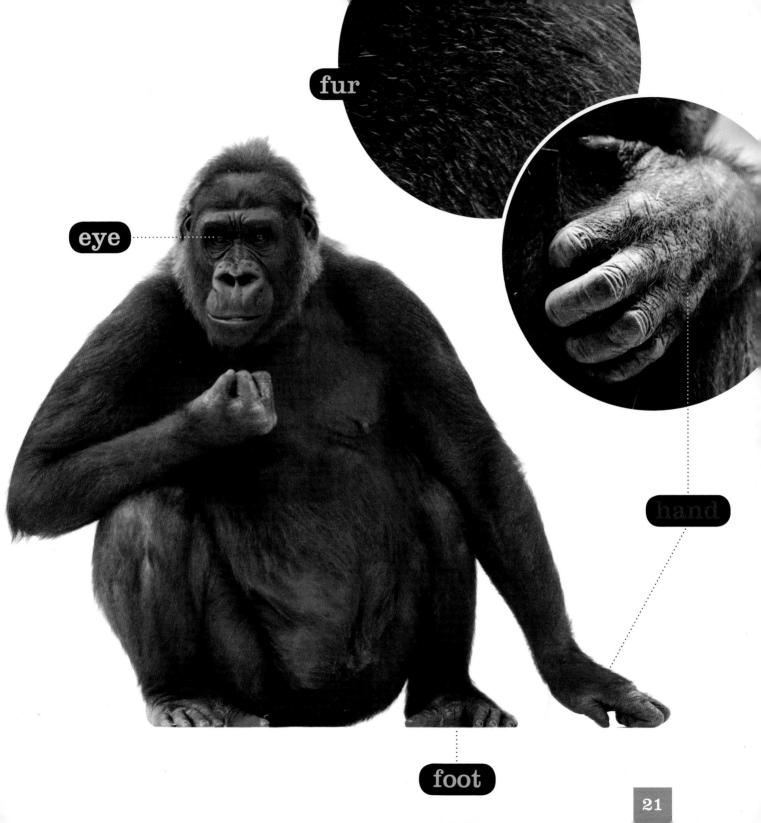

fur

eye

hand

foot

21

Words to Know

Africa: the second-biggest piece of land in the world

grunt: a low, short sound that comes from the back of the throat

jaws: the upper and lower parts of the mouth

troop: a group of gorillas that live together

Read More

Gibbons, Gail. *Gorillas*.
New York: Holiday House, 2011.

Taylor, Barbara. *Apes and Monkeys*.
New York: Kingfisher, 2004.

Websites

Koko's Kids Club
http://www.koko.org/kidsclub/
Learn more about a famous gorilla named Koko.

The Yellow Gorilla
http://www.storyplace.org/preschool/activities/
gorillaonstory.asp
Listen to a story, and find out more about what gorillas eat.

Index